SHOWBOAT

By Grace Cavalieri

SHOWBOAT
By Grace Cavalieri

Published in the United States by GOSS183

ISBN 13: 978-0-93-857260-2
ISBN-10: 0-938572-60-1

Publisher: GOSS183
Cover photo: "Reflections" by Dan Murano
Author photo: Tony Lewis
Interior illustration: Cynthia Cavalieri
Editor: April Carter Grant

www.gracecavalieri.com
www.poetsandartists.com
www.goss183.com

SHOWBOAT

Dedicated to All Navy Wives

Find out who you are then do it on purpose
...Dolly Parton

What's, after God, most friendly is the soul in love
To be within her cave.
He's waiting from above
...Angelus Silesius

The only risk is not taking a chance
...Bob Hicok

Birds   in   New Hampshire
Maria's laughing in the kitchen
All night the birds
Taped to us inside
          let them go
Pressed against the pane
          Let them

October
The year we met
Ken proved we could do anything
Even if penniless
Even if gangs of thought
were
        against us
        in accord
We could do anything
Together   in each of us

Ice on the door   he   opened
It anyway
Shadows in the cellar   then light
Years before he froze to death
            In intubation
We would dance on the floor
            before
The pipes failed   bird
If you cannot fly
            You are useless

First house was   a song in a flower
Gardenias   Japonica   Carnations
Queen Anne's Lace
I unlatched   the door
        lifted
The linoleum
Painted   the porch
Put   milk on green leaves
Made   mosaics of hours
Had a child   bought a silver cup

The dust stays in the air but
We are not there
We left traces   a fake Mondrian
In the garage   a neighbor
Feeding her dog
The coast went north and south
Telling each other this   again
            there are
Headlights on the roadway   a diaper
            A new curtain

Just past the past   to the left
We threw the rope toward us
Sand   sun   lagoon   run
Shunning memory
The wreck of the wrong
Featuring the future   See?
Birds that are not black and blue
          Still fly

Blood now   babies now
Half a body turned to make
New bodies
Harder than truth
New heads   sweet
Oh church bells   breast
Tongues of milk   against me
Give them each a hat
Say "sun" "probable" "bundle"
All the stems have leaves

Florida

We'd been here before
the Navy again
Carrying pictures shoes cribs
We had mothers been mothers
Our thumbprints women shared plates
Strange lights came through
Yet the blue water
The red birds a boat listless
Always waiting weightless water

Friends are you listening
Piercing the air with jewelry
and cocktail glasses
Crucifying death with wine
Smoke and straps music
bare shoulders
Every syllable a new friend
Cakes in the oven

The fire of it put a steak on
Join the unending sea
Feed and come and
Scrape against us painting helmets
Leave markings Party forever
Glass that does not break
Men who fly who do not die

We found cruel hands twisted the
wrong wrist
This was a mistake forget it
Alcohol dead sparrows
Cease our wonders our neighbor's
Husband raped her
She said 'good makeup protects
From sunburn' she says it does

Don't go men but you must
Barbara hid money and
polished the floors
Jenny bought pillows
Betty locked her son outside
Sandra played bridge
Men dispirited the air
With their airplanes
New weather Old weather
No one cried
Young people traveled to us

Sometimes I dream the aircraft carrier is
a showboat
With dancing girls and music
accordions
Boxes of wine and pastries too
Easter eggs and different species of fun
I wouldn't even be jealous
If he were happy
Bobbing on the waves singing laughing

Discovery   that's the word
For ships   horns   doorknobs
     we're in it now
Quiet   loud   compared to what
A blue and gold dress   left
          weeping   the mercy of arms
The trees grew larger
Each year we took the children
     Back to see them

That August a plane crashed
It was Donna's pilot   we went there
Her tan arms   her white linen dress
The knock on the door
Thank God   her door   was not our door
          Don't say that out loud
Blonde Donna who never thought
          anything bad
Now she's as human as it gets

And what of the next one and
          the jacket
You loaned her
And the soy sauce jar she gave you
Inside a circle we stood
Of what could possibly happen

Stars and Stripes Forever
Old cars   new cars
Next in line   goodbye   goodbye
Don't look back   please don't
            cry
The stalker waits
The decal on the car
Says   a   squadron went to sea

Hold our hands together
The lake is green   Whidbey Island
The children run
The wings fly   the black sand shines
Minnows   swim below the surface
Fluttering the day   every one of them

Oh heroes   Oh straps   vests   what is lowly
What is high   the air is like thick   grass
The contrails are
            resurrections
Spinning on the far side
            of the world   silent
How we keep going without a word from you
Not even a secret to keep

Yet poetry will happen   Helen
Reads   Jane Austen
Meg plays Bach on her piano
          pocketing   sounds
          Our hair blows
Tropical plants sing in dark woods
Sisters   ideas   English muffins
Tricycles   outside   Cuban missiles

Lovely children in their cribs
Wake now   remember
The moth of a mother leaning into
Your clear dark
What was left of sleep
The fountain over you
The silence we guarded
You who will never die
            Pieces of heaven

The future is crying stand up
Move like pigeons always
Going home   bringing dishes
                Forget terror
                 Nestle wherever you live
Tree shadows are everywhere
East Coast   West coast
The hilltop is just another place

What if he learns Russian and
You do not   what are the summaries
The outcomes of being left at home
What to fasten   hold in palms of your hand
What slope to climb
How do the steps go up and not down
It takes a long time

Frame this picture
Squarer of morning suns
Men with scopes   women
        with intricacies
Gusts of wind   both places
Yellow tablecloth   broken tulips
Mountains   valleys   oceans
Everyone wants to come home
Even us at home

Warm the rice   pull the fish
Swim   run   row   wear a scarf
Not poverty   not riches
Pencils   paper   then the cat gives
            birth to kittens
And the children deliver them
We are all   so scared   so numb
            It feels like joy

I was born in Trenton
And never thought of
          California
How a camper loses brakes downhill
The comfort of picnic tables
Wild horses in Montana
Bears clawing against the car
            in Wyoming
Two a.m. an army of flies
Then the blanket   the horizon
The slip   of safe cement   forgotten

Blue brocade   that's what it looked
      like   the broken light   sky
Whales migrating   Del Mar
Children   clutching   to grow
That restaurant on the sand
          a corner table
It fit all of us   the silk shore
      Click   gone

Maggie's husband crashed
A ruler was found in his plane engine
           dropped in
What inspector is missing a ruler?
Six children and seriously drunk
           she came
Her head on the table every night
The children eating grilled cheese
          Hawaii   that's her goal
She'll teach   swimming
We taught   her kids   to swim
Feed them   Feed them   Feed them

How to be selective   to live till age 50
My hair up in a barrette
          waiting
For the mailman
Shelley eats chocolate ice cream
Colleen vanilla with chocolate syrup
Cindy paints on small chairs
Angel listens as I read
      Teilhard de Chardin
Her first steps toddle to the French masters
      Running with Kazantzakis

How many times did I tell him
Yet he did   yet he would
He may die tomorrow
          so he will
No matter how we made
Tempura from scratch   swore love
He will do what he wants
Without limits   like a frightened song
popping up   impersonal   soiling your
Fingers   so true   there's no putting it back

Women have windows
From the beginning
For good reason   Mary Ellen and I flew
She drew   I imagined   not like others
We knew we were different
Naming the flood we saw   the choices
Our breath   made books   they stay

If the Landing Signal Officer
Had legs cut off from the
          wire
Snapped on the carrier
If his legs were left on the deck
We have to move again
It's only logical   cross the country
Someone has to take his place

Goodbye cliff where I could see
              the church below
High surf   Marlene dancing
Sally's   hand screened patterns
Becky's ceramic pots   traded for
        children's dental work
Artists are everywhere
        save your sight for the next ones
Thread needles without eyes
          You can do it

What if your daughter
Got a gold rose
On a gold chain from her teacher
Because her father was at sea
What if that possession got vacuumed
Up   never to be seen elsewhere
Sudden losses are everywhere
They float into machines
          a man goes
A necklace disappears

Asleep in the dark whatever may happen
He's flying over a postage stamp
Landing on a dime without a light
The phone rings a voice says
I know your husband's gone
I know you're alone
I'm watching you
We sleep huddled in one bed
I tell the skipper's wife
How many beetles are in
the field
How many are advancing
How many escape a foot

Soon it will be over this year or the next
The hurricane where we are in a motel
With water and vanilla wafers
And it was over with a husband still at sea

Once in Pensacola
Beatrice came to
Help me and said a woman in
Her neighborhood left a baby alone
crawling
On the floor all day so she could
leave to clean another woman's house
every day
and it was true
We went and looked in the window
What is sudden conviction?
Not dropping dead at
The sight?

Bribe the world to make it
Happy   cut newspaper articles
            before   you read them
So you can't see bad news
Momentum means go
Born means move
Easter hats will do it   shiny shoes
True love   maybe Christ
Will save the rest of us and our
            Cold sweat

Eve tried to stop the marks on the
World   the smudges   the
Creatures worming   out the apple
The fires inside   women   with
Bad brains/good brains   but no amount
would help change   until   they stood up
Marching   women   rain   protesting
            flushed with it
1975   potato salad   join the ranks

I remember 1958   all of us   moving
The first black family
Into Levittown   PA
I never spoke of it   before
The band around the
House   Cindy   two years old
In a stroller   bags of groceries
Could   we   do it again   no
Not with a baby in the eye
            Of a hunter

When I found my mother dead
it was morning
Unintended things happen
Even in June   if it were cold
With frost   I could understand
But June? With flowers in the lobby?

Will it ever be more than 2pm
On top of everything else   someone
Stole the rabbit   this would be
twenty years later   but the
Memory of a rabbit is still in the
Cage   that's the worst of it
He only had straw anyway

1968 all those actors tripping over
Each other   all those words
I wrote
Nasty little things   like slipping
On something in the dark
That squeaked   obscenities

Women were to speak in
The bedroom the way they
Spoke in the living room
On stage
            (we were told)
What did we do with that
To make it better
But throw sand in our eyes
            staring at clouds
Until we learned to tell the truth

Remember that I am   even   now
            searching to
See the miraculous even now
Something that will exceed
            the eyelids
Of a Navy wife   who will not leave

Then he died after all those years
            of waiting
In the snow for me
After being young with me   then old
The inlets   the muddy comforts   the
Tomorrows (so many) the hammering
            of metal
The tea   a twelve-gun-salute

Don’t feel anything   not now
                 not yet
There’s too much concurrent
                 follow
The voice in your head instead
The pressing   the spill   mirrors
And moons   green puddles
Egrets lifting   dunes receding
Don’t stop   put your hair into knots
Something wild is at work
Just another passage

On TV the people talk
They speak weeds from their lips
My feet reach the slippers
             under the bed
Their mouths say   Hope   but
Nothing comes out
             they don’t know
Once Shelley caught a fish
And Ken put it in the bathtub
For a whole week   they don’t
             Know real Hope

Where the mind can go   to an echo
Of a ladder   or the rust   from the
Water   or the fear of a clock
Or a father who is now a black/blue
Butterfly   noble and gorgeous
What a crooked circle   how lucky
               We were

Wide-eyed with hems dripping
Down the chapels   our   girls
Answer   the questions of
The priest   roses will teach
          everything I did not
War evolves   the dust of love
          petals still fresh
I didn't know how to tell them

Every house floats on air
The body out loud
Falling down the stairs or up
Walking/waking   little girls
I sent you out saying   *This Is Life*
What do you think of it
The tangled beauty   I kept for you
Whenever you returned

Moments before death
          four
Girls stood at his bed
Should we?   now   it's time
It's raining   but he can fly IFR
Instruments   pull the plug
There's really   no plug
Just five seconds   don't let
Him suffocate please   pink face
Then before I could scream
        White chalk

Let us mark this day with
            a caisson
A person with a new dress
Soup for the crowd   they came
From all over   lifted
Me up above their heads   carried
Me like the corpse   I was

Now I am alone as light
As the smell of lilacs
New roof   new cat   new fear
I can see everything from
Here   slanting   heading straight
         Inside the gate

It's better than having nothing
              to remember
              those pictures
First   I sit up   then   I lie down
Yet they stay   smiling   not lonely
Turning the unbroken   the speck
That is the heart   A medical "cat scan"
Says there's no calcium there
Brave metaphor shuffling the heart's dust

Don't think I'm sad   I am not
We took back silver on my wedding day
And traded it for pewter   we
Knew the value of the dull shine
And lived by it   everything
Else was for promotional purposes
Sounds   feelings   thoughts
I said   look at the light
            on the tree
Even down on the bark   the part
that's rotten   My God   it sparkles

Joyce just flew away one day
After all these years   what I loved
The best was how she loved me
She lay down in her skin
            like silk panties
She entrusted her words to me
She drove down a road
Never gone before
She never even looked both ways

Even now there's   something new
Emily at 94 moved to Sharpsburg
Oh West Virginia
Searching all around
The twisted snakes   the beans
I lost an opera in my computer
Vickie's cousin got it back
But all the words were in a
          different order
But how I loved my French neighbor
Solange   and her French   mushrooms

Cancel that thought
How I missed my daughter's
homecoming
Because I wanted a career
let's have a prize instead
Spinning and tipping   growth
The crust of it   the total wish
The shattering   and stacking
The mortal bread   the real
The paper cup   that looked
So full I took it for china

What we were wrapped in
Friends for life   Sabine   swimming
Upstream   the women
Burrowing secrets   opening doors
Unlock   unlock   unlock
Sally bought paint   then died
Oceans of treasures   my red shirt
Unbuttoned

I'm grown now   ancestors
Take your ancient anger with
Its attached language
your skills
Your bribes of bones
Blood from other countries
Nobody needs your rivers now

Ellen was an accountant at PBS
Linda was our secretary
She had a long fingernail,
I'm thinking it (broke and) entered us
With cocaine   home again
                    from Blues Ally
Heart pumping   only seven dollars
                    worth
My   pillow was shaking   all night
Thank God I didn't have   eight

The business world does not have
Velvet wrists   It has rubber   bayonets
It does not listen   but how I stayed
Amazed at men   always men
Rubbing their rough edges
                    advising
Surprising   conjuring   pretending
Washing up   to begin again

I caused no trouble and did my job
When asked I said clean words
I wore a white shirt
                once I
Didn't see a mountain and
Walked into it twelve times
Give me a fighting chance and
It could be thirteen

Cindy's in college now   Cindy's an artist
Cindy needs me now
But I didn't know it
I was watching hidden places
In the world   I was belonging
To cascades   high heels and New York City
On Friday

1970 I forgot to say   Antioch College
the first time teaching my art
my name
Fell away from me and
I was new   moment by moment
Students like fish coming to the surface
Every sky was starry from teaching
My long skirt turning wider

Start something   Glen Echo Park
Ken will empty the swimming pool
And fill it with sculpture
bats flew
Through broken windows   poets sat
Like bells   about to ring   ideas
And callings   a basket of knitting
At the feet of women writing

Where was everyone else
          where
Should I have been
Teaching? Cooking?
            no I was
Confronting life's translations
Moving toward the capable
But should I have
Taught Angel something besides
Making tacos   if I could strip
My skin   would I find
        What I did not do?

Anita asked my husband
To spend the night
She, my friend!   He said No   I
Didn't know people did that   friends
Fading marriage   fading dreams
Naked people   the land and the sea
     Are   lonelier than I thought

What does it take to forget again
The precious barriers
              do not
Build a door in your office and we
Will sell the condo   this way we can
Hammer a new home in the woods
And take our history with us and
              leave
Our history without us

Intense woods
I didn't like your gnats
Four butterflies per leaf
        I admit
Fern too   gravel like marriage crunching
Beneath us   summer days   but
Look what you built   just look
Gleaming statues   Ken
Five acres of metal   rising

And the music
Vickie heard it in her
Head   it just happened
        nobody ever
Died of it   it was intact
        what
Else could I do but put it
        into words
Words hanging on her clothes line
Shimmering with embarrassment
Until the wisdom of melody
Washed them clean

Oh the voice sounded scared alright
On the radio
                mine   like I was
Begging for forgiveness
                but soon I
Found serious fun forgetting
The poets were all required and
                rewarded
The poets' voices   putting
The world   back together
For everyone   to hear
    No sense wearing a   bow on radio

Rereading this I forget to be
thankful
How could I a frightened
Traveler be given so much
Should I list his love
Once he cupped
my chin in his hand
How could he be dead
If his clothes
Hang in the closet and every day
I lay out a clean shirt in
Case it's needed

Above all else
I love my children, not charms
But the bracelet
Relentless like fashions of art or games
Personal and compassionate
Shelley and Colleen laugh
always at ease
Understanding Cindy and Angel
each young clear
Unforeseen events beauty
Even that didn't stop them

New Hampshire
This story I'm telling
It's cracked from the course of time
It's just the brink of the abyss
follies of stained glass
A wonderful pleasure
Crimson ribbons a minute's silence

40383895R00021

Made in the USA
Middletown, DE
28 March 2019